Contents

DEFENDING

The main aims of defence are to prevent your opponents reaching the goal and to gain possession of the ball yourself. These two aims require the combined efforts of all team members.

PAGE 5

ATTACKING

The aim of the game is to score more goals than the opposition. That means attacking! Attack starts when you obtain the ball and ends with the shot at goal.

PAGE 11

PLAYING OFF THE BALL

Not every player can have the ball at the same time. So players must know how to play when they do not have the ball.

PAGE 17

TACTICS

In order to win, the attack must overcome the defence. Attackers can go through alone or in combinations of two or three. These combinations have to be well practised in training.

PAGE 20

ONE-AGAINST-ONE

On the pitch it's eleven against eleven. But it's the individuals who make the vital difference to the game. Individual confrontation is the commonest form of play.

PAGE 25

DEAD-BALL SITUATIONS

When starting with a dead-ball - at a corner or a free kick - it is possible to prepare and predict the course of play and to rehearse it.

PAGE 30

Text by Didier Braun / Artwork by Claude-Henri Julliard / Scenario by André Manguin

Also published by Corgi Books:
TENNIS
WINDSURFING
JUDO

FOOTBALL

A CORGI BOOK 0 552 542741

PRINTING HISTORY

First published in France by Chancerel Editions
Corgi edition published in Great Britain 1986

Copyright © in text and illustrations
Chancerel Editions 1984

All rights reserved. No part of this publication
may be reproduced, stored in a retrieval system
or transmitted, in any form or by any means
electronic, mechanical, photocopying, recording,
or otherwise, without the prior permission
of the Copyright owner.

Corgi Books are published by Transworld Publishers Ltd.,
61-63 Uxbridge Road, Ealing, London W5 5SA.

Printed in Italy by ROTOLITO LOMBARDA S.p.A., Milan, Italy

1

DEFENDING

THE MAIN AIMS OF DEFENCE ARE TO PREVENT YOUR OPPONENTS REACHING THE GOAL AND TO GAIN POSSESSION OF THE BALL YOURSELF. THESE TWO AIMS REQUIRE THE COMBINED EFFORTS OF ALL TEAM MEMBERS.

MARKING PRESENTS PHYSICAL AND MENTAL PROBLEMS TO THE OPPONENT WHO'S MARKED AND ALSO HIS TEAM-MATE WHO HAS THE BALL.

THIS CHAP'S ALWAYS BEHIND ME! I CAN NEVER GET AWAY FROM HIM.

WHO CAN I PASS TO?

LOOSE MARKING CAN GIVE A GOAL AWAY. THE CENTRAL STRIKER HAS TOO MUCH...

...ROOM, AND THE MIDFIELDER WITH THE BALL HAS AN EASY CHOICE.

THE STRIKER GATHERS THE "THROUGH" PASS UNCHALLENGED AND THEN SHOOTS.

DEFENDING

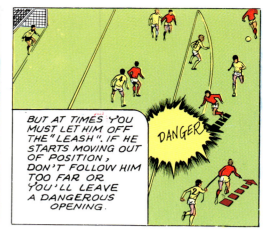

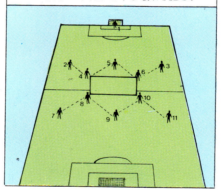
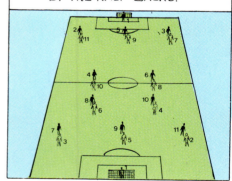

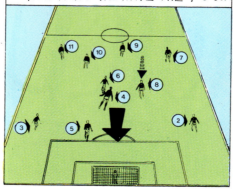

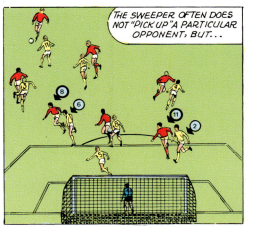
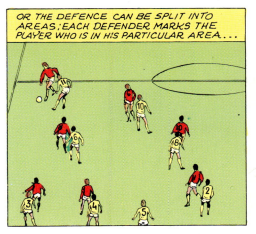

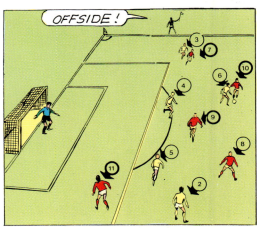

DEFENDING

THE MODERN TREND IS TO COMBINE THE BEST OF THE DIFFERENT DEFENCE SYSTEMS. YOU MUST KNOW HOW TO USE THE SECURITY PROVIDED BY STRICT MARKING BY THE BACKS, AND BY A SWEEPER WHO COVERS THEM.

MID-FIELD PLAYERS MUST COVER THE WHOLE OF THEIR AREA... THEY MUST REINFORCE OUR LAST LINE OF DEFENCE.

DEFENCE OF YOUR GOAL BEGINS AS SOON AS THE OTHER SIDE HAS THE BALL.

TRY TO WRECK YOUR OPPONENTS' BUILD-UP BY PUTTING PRESSURE ON THE ONE WHO HAS THE BALL AND HIS PARTNERS. YOUR ATTACKERS MUST CHANGE THEIR ROLE.

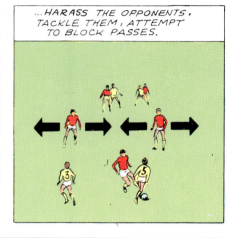
...HARASS THE OPPONENTS, TACKLE THEM, ATTEMPT TO BLOCK PASSES.

YOUR MIDFIELDERS MUST BE READY TO TAKE ADVANTAGE OF THE PRESSURE APPLIED BY YOUR FORWARDS.

MID FIELDERS - STAY CLOSE TO THE MEN YOU'RE MARKING WHEN THEY'VE GOT THE BALL, OR WHEN YOU THINK THEY'RE LIKELY TO GET IT!

LEARN TO PRESSURISE THE BALL WHEN YOUR OPPONENT IS DRIBBLING THE BALL TOWARDS YOU. IF YOU TACKLE TOO SOON HE MAY BREAK THROUGH YOUR DEFENSIVE SCREEN.

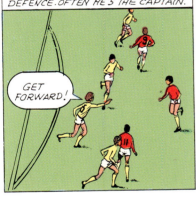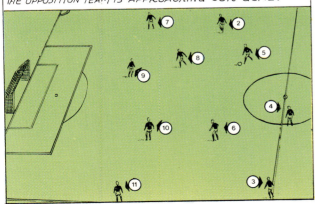

DEFENDING

TACKLING INVOLVES A RISK. ONLY TACKLE WHEN YOU ARE SURE OF WINNING THE BALL. IF YOU DON'T WIN THE BALL YOU COULD LET YOUR OPPONENT THROUGH TO...

...A DANGEROUS POSITION. AT ALL TIMES A TEAM-MATE SHOULD TRY TO GIVE YOU COVER.

IN BEATING YOU, THE OPPONENT CAN KNOCK THE BALL TOO FAR AHEAD OF HIMSELF; THEN YOUR TEAM-MATE CAN SWOOP IN.

WHEN THERE'S AN IMMEDIATE THREAT TO YOUR GOAL YOU MUST CLEAR THE BALL FROM THE DANGER ZONE. PLAY THE BALL HIGH, WIDE AND LONG.

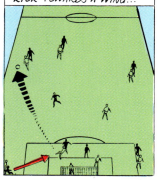

EVEN SO, YOU MUST TRY TO TURN THIS TO YOUR ADVANTAGE. FOR EXAMPLE KICK TOWARDS A WING...

...AND SET UP AN ATTACK. YOUR FORWARDS SHOULD ANTICIPATE THIS AND MOVE INTO POSITION TO COLLECT YOUR CLEARANCE.

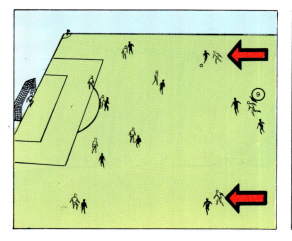

THERE ARE TIMES WHEN YOU ARE HARD-PRESSED. THE TEMPTATION IS TO PULL EVERYONE BACK. BUT A PLAYER CAN STAY UP FRONT AND FORM A THREAT OF COUNTER-ATTACK.

STAY BACK, WE MUST WATCH HIM!

THERE ARE SEVERAL ATTACKING FORMATIONS:
a) 2 WINGERS AND 2 CENTRE-FORWARDS
b) 1 WINGER AND 2 CENTRE-FORWARDS
c) 2 WINGERS AND 1 CENTRE-FORWARD
d) 2 CENTRE FORWARDS.

ATTACKING

THE AIM OF THE GAME IS TO SCORE MORE GOALS THAN THE OPPOSITION. THAT MEANS ATTACKING! ATTACK STARTS WHEN YOU OBTAIN THE BALL AND ENDS WITH THE SHOT AT GOAL.

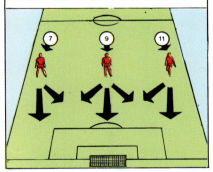

THIS CLASSIC ARRANGEMENT OF ATTACKERS IS AS FOLLOWS: ONE CENTRE-FORWARD — OR STRIKER — AND TWO WINGERS, SPANNING THE WHOLE WIDTH OF THE FIELD.

THEY PLAY AN OPEN GAME, UTILISING THE SIDES OF THE PITCH.

THIS ARRANGEMENT ALLOWS THEM TO PULL DEFENCES WIDE, CREATING SPACE IN THE CENTRE.

A TEAM MAY HAVE JUST ONE WINGER AND TWO STRIKERS.

THE EMPTY WING ALLOWS THE MIDFIELDERS AND FULL-BACKS TO COME THROUGH.

OFTEN ONE OPENS GAPS FOR THE OTHER OR FORMS A PIVOT TO PROVIDE A RETURN PASS.

2 ATTACKING

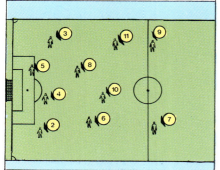
CONSTANTLY REINFORCING THE MID-FIELD MEANS THAT A LOT OF TEAMS PLAY WITH JUST TWO STRIKERS.

THIS ARRANGEMENT IS PARTICULARLY USEFUL IN A COUNTER-ATTACK. ANOTHER THING...

...THAT IS NECESSARY FOR THIS **ARRANGEMENT** IS THAT THE MID-FIELD PLAYERS MUST BE ABLE TO TURN INTO STRIKERS WHEN THEIR TEAM HAVE THE BALL.

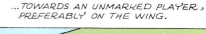
WE START ATTACKING AS SOON AS WE'VE GOT POSSESSION OF THE BALL. AND THAT INCLUDES THE GOALKEEPER. WHEN THE OPPOSITION ARE ALREADY MOVING BACK, HE SHOULD THROW THE BALL.

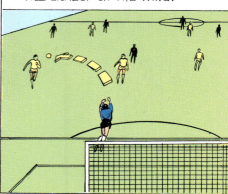
...TOWARDS AN UNMARKED PLAYER, PREFERABLY ON THE WING.

BUT IF THERE'S AN UNMARKED PLAYER WELL UPFIELD, IT'S OFTEN ADVISABLE TO KICK THE BALL TOWARDS HIM.

TOO OFTEN WE SEE A GOALKEEPER WHO HAS JUST PULLED OFF A GOOD SAVE MAKE A MESS OF CLEARING THE BALL.

THE MOST ACCURATE METHOD, BUT THE ONE WHICH NEEDS THE BEST CO-ORDINATION, IS THE DROP-KICK.

HIT THE BALL JUST AFTER IT HAS BOUNCED... THAT GIVES A GREATER MOMENTUM. THE BALL MUST BE HIT WITH THE INSTEP.

2 ATTACKING

Forwards should have one aim above all: to score goals.

The mid-field men must help the forwards' play by giving them support.
Also they must exploit gaps...

...opened up in the opponents' defence by their forwards luring men out of position...

...and move on to the wing when the winger moves to the centre.

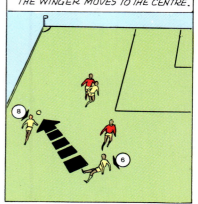

Midfielders are fetchers...

...and carriers. They set the forwards in motion.

But their job isn't limited to passing... they must follow through.

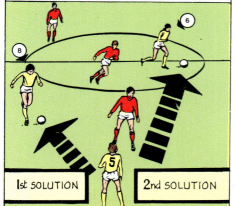

1st SOLUTION   2nd SOLUTION

YOU MUST TRY ANYTHING THAT WILL GET YOU INTO A SCORING POSITION. DEVELOP A SPRINT START.

LEARN TO BRING THE BALL UNDER CONTROL QUICKLY. USE YOUR CHEST AT TIMES.

IF YOU WANT TO SUCCEED IN A MATCH, **PRACTISE** YOUR MOVES A HUNDRED TIMES IN TRAINING.

BRING IT DOWN.

WITH SPEED AND BALL-CONTROL YOU CAN USE THE WING AND GET BEHIND THE DEFENCE. FOLLOW UP...

...WITH A CENTRE FROM THE BY-LINE. THE RECIPIENT OF YOUR CROSS SHOULD TIME HIS RUN...

...PERFECTLY, AS DEFENCES RARELY ALLOW A STATIONARY MAN A SHOT.

A PASS IN THE ATTACKING AREA MUST BE BOTH FAST AND ACCURATE SO THAT THE RECIPIENT CAN CONTROL IT IMMEDIATELY.

FINALLY, IT MUST TAKE DEFENDERS BY SURPRISE.

2 ATTACKING

IN DESCRIBING GOALS WE TOO OFTEN FORGET THE FINAL PASS WHICH MADE THE SCORING SHOT POSSIBLE.

THIS PASS, WHICH AT THE TIME MOVES THE BALL ACCURATELY AND ALSO GETS RID OF YOUR PARTNER'S MARKER, CAN BE MADE FORWARDS...

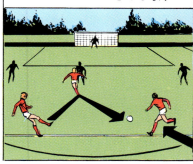

...OR, IF YOU HAVE YOUR BACK TO THE GOAL, BACKWARDS TO A PLAYER IN SUPPORT.

SHOOTING AT THE GOAL IS THE MOST IMPORTANT SKILL. STRONG MOTIVATION TO SCORE IS VITAL.

DETERMINATION — BALL CONTROL — BALANCE

ALERTNESS — STRENGTH

KEEP TRYING! SHOOTING NEEDS MUCH PRACTICE!

IN MODERN FOOTBALL THE STRIKER'S JOB IS MORE AND MORE DIFFICULT AS THEY FACE INCREASINGLY WELL-ORGANISED DEFENCES.

YOU'VE JUST SCORED FOUR OUT OF FIVE SHOTS! NOW YOU MUST MAKE IT FIVE OUT OF FIVE.

A TEAM CAN OFTEN PLAY VERY WELL, BUT IT WON'T SUCCEED UNLESS IT HAS **THAT** RARE INDIVIDUAL WHO HAS AN INSATIABLE HUNGER FOR GOALS.

REMEMBER THAT THE MAJORITY OF SHOOTING CHANCES COME FROM BALLS THAT ARE BOUNCING, SO PRACTISE VOLLEYS AND HALF-VOLLEYS.

3

PLAYING OFF THE BALL

NOT EVERY PLAYER CAN HAVE THE BALL AT THE SAME TIME. SO PLAYERS MUST KNOW HOW TO PLAY WHEN THEY DO NOT HAVE THE BALL.

TEAM-MATES CAN'T ALWAYS READ YOUR MIND, SO YOU MUST CALL FOR THE BALL. A SUDDEN CHANGE OF DIRECTION CAN CONFUSE YOUR TEAM AS WELL AS THE OPPOSITION.

ENSURE YOU ARE WELL-PLACED TO TAKE A PASS AND THAT YOU CAN BREAK FREE OF YOUR MARKER.

MANY TEAMS EMPLOY TWO CENTRE-BACKS, WORKING CLOSELY TOGETHER TO GUARD THE VITAL PATH TO THE GOAL.

PULLING THEM OUT OF POSITION CAN BE THE KEY TO WINNING A GAME.

THE SECRET IS TO HOOK THEM. DON'T BE AFRAID TO LURE THEM TOWARDS YOUR OWN GOAL.

3 PLAYING OFF THE BALL

ONE MAN BREAKING AWAY LEAVES ONLY ONE OPTION.

IF SEVERAL BREAK THERE CAN BE THREE OPTIONS...

...OR EVEN FOUR.

YOUR BREAKING AWAY TO RECEIVE A PASS MAY BE IGNORED BUT...

...DON'T BE ANNOYED BECAUSE IT CAN CREATE A USEFUL SPACE IN THE DEFENCE.

HERE A PLAYER CALLS FOR THE BALL, EITHER TO GO IT ALONE...

...DOWN THE WING... OR TO OPEN UP THE DEFENCE.

IT'S IMPERATIVE TO RESPOND QUICKLY TO A CALL, PARTICULARLY WHEN IT COMES FROM THE WINGS.

AN ACCURATE LONG BALL OVER THE HEADS OF DEFENDERS — OR AROUND THEM.

TRY TO PLACE YOUR KICK SO THAT THE WINGER DOES NOT HAVE TO BREAK STRIDE.

4

TACTICS

IN ORDER TO WIN, THE ATTACK MUST OVERCOME THE DEFENCE. ATTACKERS CAN GO THROUGH ALONE OR IN COMBINATIONS OF TWO OR THREE. THESE COMBINATIONS HAVE TO BE WELL PRACTISED IN TRAINING.

TWO PLAYERS CROSSING IN FRONT OF A TEAM-MATE WITH THE BALL CREATE SPACE AND CAUSE CONFUSION AMONGST...

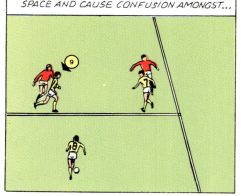

... THE OPPOSITION. THE PLAYER WITH THE BALL HAS THREE CHOICES.

HE CAN EITHER PASS TO YOU OR TAKE THE BALL THROUGH HIMSELF.

No. 6 HAS THE BALL. HIS FORWARDS MOVE TOWARDS HIM OR SIDEWAYS...

...TO THE RIGHT, OPENING UP A GAP ON THE LEFT-WING INTO WHICH...

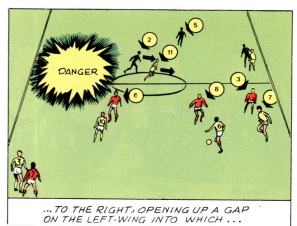

... A FULL-BACK, No. 3, RUNS, NOW ACTING AS A WINGER.

WINGERS EXCHANGING POSITIONS CAN BE A DEADLY VARIATION OF THE CROSS-OVER TACTIC.

MIDFIELDER No. 6 AND CENTRE-FORWARD PASS TO EACH OTHER WHILE THEIR WINGMEN SWITCH; THEN THE BALL IS...

...DRIVEN TO THE ONE WITH MOST ROOM.

THE BASIC COMBINATION IS THE ONE-TWO.

No. 10 DRAWS HIS MAN, SHORT PASSES THE BALL TO HIS TEAM-MATE...

...THEN RUNS AROUND THE OPPONENT TO COLLECT A FIRST-TIME RETURN PASS.

IT'S DIFFICULT TO USE THE ONE-TWO NEAR THE OPPOSING GOAL WHERE THERE ARE TOO MANY DEFENDERS.

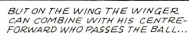

BUT ON THE WING THE WINGER CAN COMBINE WITH HIS CENTRE-FORWARD WHO PASSES THE BALL...

...BACK INTO THE LINE OF HIS RUN. THE FULL-BACK IS BEATEN.

THE ONE-TWO IS A PRECISE MOVE; THE FIRST PASS MUST BE ACCURATE AND HARD-HIT, OR THE DEFENDER CAN INTERCEPT.

THE RECIPIENT MUST GET CLEAR OF HIS OPPONENT BY MOVING TOWARDS HIS PARTNER.

THEN HE PASSES THE BALL BACK JUST AHEAD OF THE RUNNING PLAYER.

4 TACTICS

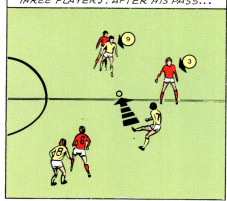

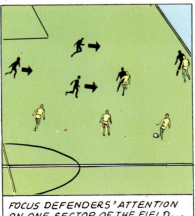
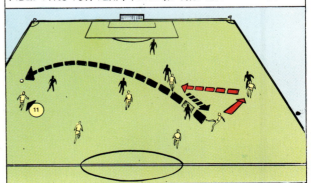

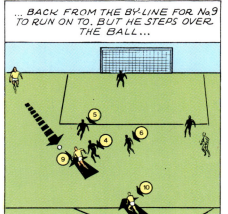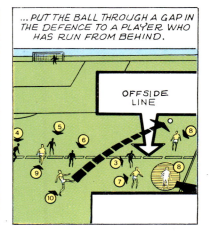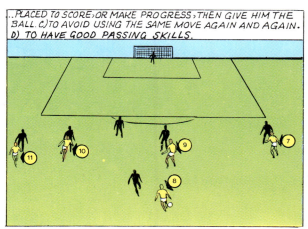

5

ONE-AGAINST-ONE

ON THE PITCH IT'S ELEVEN AGAINST ELEVEN. BUT IT'S THE INDIVIDUALS WHO MAKE THE VITAL DIFFERENCE TO THE GAME. INDIVIDUAL CONFRONTATION IS THE COMMONEST FORM OF PLAY.

FOOTBALL IS A TEAM GAME; BUT A LOT OF SITUATIONS PUT TWO PLAYERS FACE TO FACE.

THE PHYSICAL AND MENTAL ABILITIES OF DIRECT OPPONENTS ARE TESTED.

A PLAYER OFTEN MEETS THE SAME OPPONENT. COMPETITION IS KEENER THE CLOSER THEY GET TO THE GOAL.

THE SUPERIORITY OF ONE OVER THE OTHER CAN DECIDE THE SUCCESS OR FAILURE OF A TEAM.

5 ONE-AGAINST-ONE

DRIBBLING MEANS TAKING A RISK. IF A BACK LOSES THE BALL, HE COULD GIVE AWAY A GOAL!

DRIBBLING IS MAINLY FOR ATTACK.

DON'T DRIBBLE IN YOUR PENALTY AREA!

DRIBBLING AIMS TO UNBALANCE YOUR OPPONENT. YOU CAN MOVE TO THE RIGHT THEN...

...HOOK WITH THE OUTSIDE OF THE LEFT FOOT. THIS BODY FEINT AND CHANGE OF DIRECTION...

...CAUSES THE OPPONENT TO STUMBLE.

OR YOU CAN INVITE A TACKLE BY KNOCKING THE BALL FROM ONE FOOT TO ANOTHER.

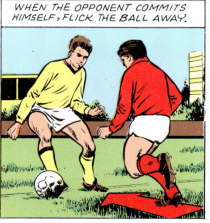

WHEN THE OPPONENT COMMITS HIMSELF, FLICK THE BALL AWAY.

THEN SWOOP ON TO IT AND ACCELERATE AWAY - FAST.

GOOD BALL CONTROL, MOVEMENT, SPEED, AND A SENSE OF BALANCE ARE THE WEAPONS OF A DRIBBLER.

EXTREMELY FAST BALL CONTROL OFTEN ALLOWS HIM TO SHOW A CLEAN PAIR OF HEELS.

A COMBINATION OF THESE ESSENTIALS CAN TANGLE UP A DEFENDER.

IF THE PLAYER WITH THE BALL IS BEING OVERTAKEN, HE CAN...

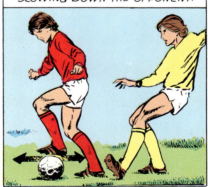
...PASS HIS FOOT OVER THE BALL, FEIGNING STOPPING, SLOWING DOWN HIS OPPONENT.

HE GIVES THE BALL ANOTHER KICK AND RESUMES HIS RUN.

ANOTHER DRIBBLE TO TRY, CALLED THE "LITTLE BRIDGE":

PASS THE BALL BETWEEN YOUR OPPONENT'S LEGS, THEN PICK IT UP AGAIN.

IN THE "BIG BRIDGE" SEND THE BALL ROUND ONE SIDE WHILE YOU GO PAST ON THE OTHER.

5 ONE-AGAINST-ONE

YOUR TACKLER SUSPECTS YOU WILL CHANGE DIRECTION...

...SO ALTER YOUR TACTIC IN A SPLIT-SECOND.

GO THE WAY YOU DIDN'T ORIGINALLY INTEND.

IF A DEFENDER HAS TO FACE A DRIBBLING OPPONENT IT'S BECAUSE HE'S ALREADY LOST ONE CONTEST: PREVENTING... ...THE OPPONENT FROM GETTING TO THE BALL.

HE MUST ALWAYS KEEP GOAL-SIDE OF HIS MAN.

HE PRESENTS A BIG OBSTACLE, FACE TO FACE.

BE AGGRESSIVE. ALL WEIGHT MUST BE BEHIND THE TACKLING FOOT.

BUT, THE GREATEST CRIME IN THE WORLD IS...

THE OVER-THE-TOP TACKLE.

A WINGER TRIES TO CUT IN WITH THE BALL AND SHOOT OR CROSS.

HE'LL TRY TO GET ROUND THE BACK AND GO FOR THE BY-LINE.

BETTER TO CONCEDE A THROW-IN THAN ALLOW HIM THROUGH.

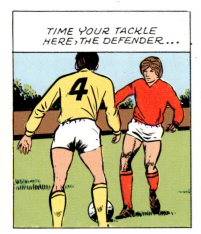

6

DEAD-BALL SITUATIONS

WHEN STARTING WITH A DEAD-BALL – AT A CORNER OR A FREE KICK – IT IS POSSIBLE TO PREPARE AND PREDICT THE COURSE OF PLAY AND TO REHEARSE IT.

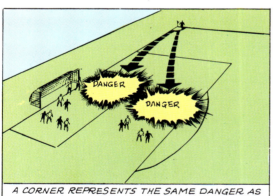

A CORNER REPRESENTS THE SAME DANGER AS A CENTRED BALL. THE 'KEEPER SHOULD BE STATIONED AT THE POST FURTHEST FROM THE KICKER.

HE AVOIDS BEING BEATEN BY...

...THE LOBBED BALL AND IS BETTER PLACED TO BEAT OUT OR CATCH OTHER TYPES OF CROSSES.

THE 'KEEPER MUST PLACE HIS DEFENDERS.

MOST FORWARDS POSITION THEMSELVES WHERE THEY CAN RUN ON TO THE BALL. IT'S OFTEN GOOD POLICY TO PLACE ONE FORWARD WHO CAN BE THE FIRST TO THE BALL FROM A CORNER PLAYED CLOSE TO GOAL.

DEFENDERS SHOULD CLOSE-MARK THE STRIKERS. ANY ON THE GOAL-LINE SHOULD STAY THERE IF THE GOALKEEPER HAS TO LEAVE IT TO GO FOR THE CROSS.

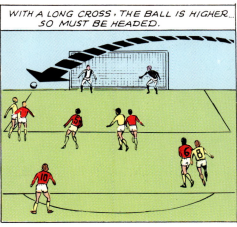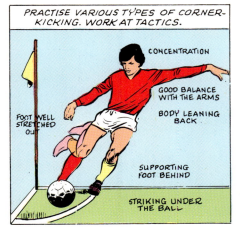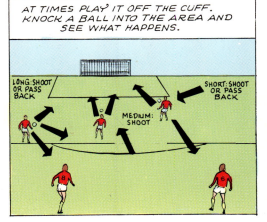

6 DEAD-BALL SITUATIONS

SOME PLAYERS HAVE PERFECTED A SPECIAL KICK FROM THE CORNER. THIS REQUIRES GREAT SKILL AND MUCH PRACTICE.

A DIRECT CORNER IS OFTEN DUE TO MISTAKES BY DEFENDERS OR THE 'KEEPER.
DEFENCE UNDER PRESSURE
GOALKEEPER OUT OF POSITION

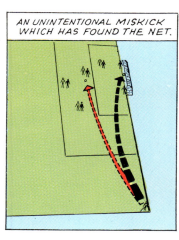
AN UNINTENTIONAL MISKICK WHICH HAS FOUND THE NET.

FREE KICK. TWO THINGS TO AVOID: AN EMPTY SPACE OR A WALL WHICH BLOCKS THE 'KEEPER'S VIEW.

THE 'KEEPER OFTEN BUILDS THE WALL. BUT IT IS BETTER IF A FORWARD PLAYER LINES IT UP LEAVING THE 'KEEPER TO CONCENTRATE ON STOPPING THE SHOT.

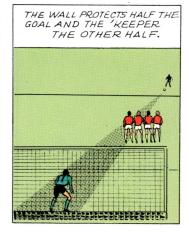
THE WALL PROTECTS HALF THE GOAL AND THE 'KEEPER THE OTHER HALF.

THE WIDTH OF THE WALL DEPENDS ON THE ANGLE...

...AND THE DISTANCE...

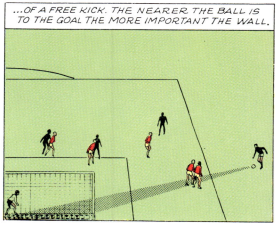
...OF A FREE KICK. THE NEARER THE BALL IS TO THE GOAL THE MORE IMPORTANT THE WALL.

IF AN INDIRECT FREE-KICK IS GIVEN AGAINST YOU IN THE...

...PENALTY AREA, EVERYBODY FORMS A WALL. IF THE SHOT...

...BEATS THE KEEPER ONE OF HIS MEN MAY MAKE A SAVE.

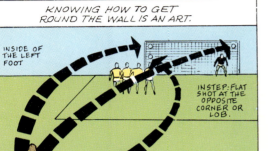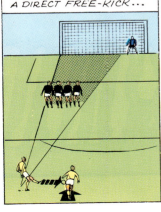

6 DEAD-BALL SITUATIONS

YOU CAN LOB THE BALL OVER THE WALL FOR A TEAM-MATE TO RUN ON TO.

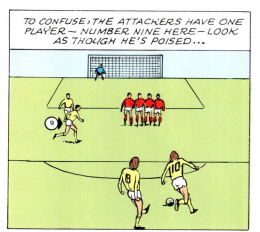
TO CONFUSE, THE ATTACKERS HAVE ONE PLAYER — NUMBER NINE HERE — LOOK AS THOUGH HE'S POISED...

...TO GO FOR THE BALL...

...BUT SEND ANOTHER — NUMBER TEN HERE — RUNNING THROUGH INSTEAD.

EACH SIDE MUST STRIVE TO OUTWIT THE OTHER. AT FREE-KICKS DON'T ALWAYS ADVERTISE THE KICKER....

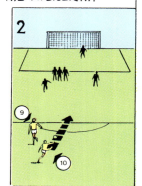

TWO OR THREE PLAYERS CAN TAKE PART IN THE PRETENCE.

THE DEFENDERS HAVE THE PROBLEM OF WORKING OUT WHICH IS TO TAKE THE KICK.

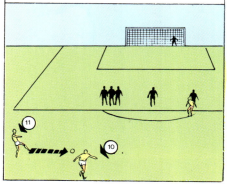
FROM A FREE-KICK A BIT OFF-CENTRE, ONE MAN PASSES TO ANOTHER... THE DEFENDERS EXPECT HIM TO SHOOT.

HE RETURNS THE PASS, DOWN THE WING... THE DEFENCE IS CAUGHT ON THE HOP AND THE WINGER CAN SHOOT OR CENTRE.

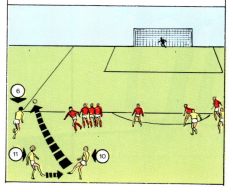
TRY A SIMILAR RUSE WITH A THIRD MAN. NOW PRACTISE THE TIPS IN THIS BOOK. THE HARD WORK IS JUST BEGINNING!